Holiday Lights

Katie Peters

GRL Consultant Diane Craig,
Certified Literacy Specialist

Pull Ahead Readers

Lerner Publications ◆ Minneapolis

Note from a GRL Consultant
This Pull Ahead leveled book has been carefully designed for beginning readers. A team of guided reading literacy experts has reviewed and leveled the book to ensure readers pull ahead and experience success.

Lerner Publications
An imprint of Lerner Publishing Group, Inc.
241 First Avenue North
Minneapolis, MN 55401 USA

For reading levels and more information, look up this title at www.lernerbooks.com.

Main body text set in Memphis Pro 24/39
Typeface provided by Linotype.

Photo Acknowledgments
The images in this book are used with the permission of: © Ailisa/Shutterstock, p. 3; © nimito/Shutterstock, pp. 4–5; © StockImageFactory.com/Shutterstock, pp. 6–7; © chomplearn/Shutterstock, pp. 8–9, 16 (middle); © Pixel-Shot/Shutterstock, pp. 10–11; © SeventyFour/Shutterstock, pp. 12–13, 16 (left); © Antipina Natalia/Shutterstock, pp. 14–15, 16 (right).

Front cover: © Drazen Zigic/Shutterstock

Library of Congress Cataloging-in-Publication Data

Names: Peters, Katie author
Title: Holiday lights / written by Katie Peters.
Description: Minneapolis : Lerner Publications, [2026] | Series: Pull ahead readers. Let's look at families. Nonfiction | Includes index. | Audience: Ages 4–7 | Audience: Grades K–1 | Summary: "Everyone celebrates different holidays, but one thing most holidays and families share is lights. Leveled text and bright photographs help readers learn about family traditions. Pairs with the fiction story, Family Time"—Provided by publisher.
Identifiers: LCCN 2025011162 (print) | LCCN 2025011163 (ebook) | ISBN 9798765689875 lib. bdg. | ISBN 9798348028596 pbk | ISBN 9798765695142 epub
Subjects: LCSH: Lighting—Social aspects—Juvenile literature | Lighting—Special effects—Juvenile literature | Christmas lights—Juvenile literature
Classification: LCC GT440 .P46 2026 (print) | LCC GT440 (ebook) | DDC 394.26028/4—dc23/eng/20250526

LC record available at https://lccn.loc.gov/2025011162
LC ebook record available at https://lccn.loc.gov/2025011163

Manufactured in the United States of America
1 – CG – 12/15/25

Table of Contents

Holiday Lights

We put lights on the tree.

We light oil lamps.

We hang red lanterns.

We light eight candles.

We light seven candles.

Many holidays have lights.

Did You See It?

candle

lantern

mitten

Index